Arc de Triomphe

Anne **Muratori-Philip**

ÉDITIONS DU PATRIMOINE

CENTRE DES
MONUMENTS NATIONAUX

Two hundred and eighty-four steps to conquer Paris! At 50 metres from the ground, the French capital reveals all its history and the most beautiful view in the world—the magical 3-kilometre stretch between the Arc de Triomphe and the Louvre with the Champs-Élysées, the obelisk of Place de la Concorde, the Jardin des Tuileries, the Arc de Triomphe du Carrousel, and the Musée du Louvre's pyramid for milestones. To the right of the Champs-Élysées is the vast glass roof of the Grand Palais, then the gleaming dome of the Invalides that steals the limelight of the Pantheon, a little further in the distance, and a huge spire in metallic lace and an integral part of Paris, the Eiffel Tower.

In the distance, behind the Louvre are the splendid Gothic structures Notre-Dame and the Tour Saint-Jacques.

To the left, perched on its hilltop, is Sacré-Coeur.

And when you turn round, you travel through history to 1989, to pass under the Grande Arche de la Défense—with a glance to the left towards Mont Valérien, a reminder of one of the most painful moments in the recent history of Paris.

At the foot of the monument is the former Place de l'Étoile, which was renamed Place Charles-de-Gaulle in 1970. An impressive sun, glorified by the twelve converging avenues and the perpetual counterclockwise motion of traffic—as if it dreamt of impeding the movement of time.

Napoleon's promise

Emperor Napoleon I was invested in disrupting time and its rules as soon as he was crowned in 1804. He wanted to assert

West façade of the Arc de Triomphe. *Facing Avenue de la Grande-Armée.* On the left, *The Conquest of Alexandria* figures on the upper relief with *Peace* below. On the right, *Crossing the Arcole Bridge* figures on the upper relief with *The Resistance* below. *The Return of the Armies* adorns the entablature frieze.

A brief history of the Arc de Triomphe

his legitimacy by marking his reign with the seal of architecture. For him, "men are only as great as the monuments they leave behind" (Jean Tulard, *Nouvelle histoire de Paris*, 1983, 71).

The victory at Austerlitz on 2 December 1805 gave him the opportunity, if only to keep the promise made to his soldiers, victors of the Austrian and Russian armies: "You will return home under triumphal arches!" (declaration by Napoleon published in *Bulletin de la Grande Armée*, 2 December 1805). Napoleon thus became part of the tradition of the Roman Empire that glorified its heroes by building such arches, a legacy taken up by all of Europe during the Renaissance. The symbol of triumphal entry, from then on the arch occupied an important place in architecture celebrating great events. It could be temporary—an ordinary wooden frame covered with painted canvases and banners—or built of stone to traverse the centuries as a witness to history.

Napoleon's promise to his troops was fulfilled on 18 February 1806. The emperor signed the decree for the construction of a triumphal arch to the glory of his armies near the site of the former Bastille prison.

The choice of site seemed logical as the district was in need of a complete redevelopment following the demolition of the fortress. And the site coincided with the armies' point of departure and return east of Paris. But the interior minister, Jean-Baptiste Nompère de Champagny, was not terribly enthusiastic. He appointed a committee of experts made up of architects and sculptors, all members of the Institut de France. Their mission was to come to a decision about the type of arch to build and, above all, find a better site on which to build it.

Several sites were discussed but none was unanimously approved. In his report to the emperor, Champagny decided in favour of the tollgate at Étoile, one of the gates enabling the crossing of the wall of the Farmers General erected in 1784: "This place is, in a way, part of the most beautiful district of Paris since it is joined by the esplanade of the Champs-Élysées. A triumphal arch will close in the most majestic and picturesque way the superb vista that we have of the Tuileries Palace . . . It will inspire the admiration of the traveller entering Paris, for monuments of this type make a greater impression at a distance by leaving the imagination great room to

manoeuvre. It will leave the person going away from the capital with a profound souvenir of its incomparable beauty. Although a long way away, he will always be in front of the Triumphant General. Your Majesty will cross it when going to Malmaison, Saint-Germain, Saint-Cloud, and even Versailles" (Jean-Baptiste Nompère de Champagny, *Rapport à l'empereur et roi concernant l'emplacement de l'Arc de Triomphe*, April 1806. Angers: Bibliothèque Municipale, MS 1277).

Convinced, Napoleon opted for Place de l'Étoile on 9 May 1806. Thus, from the central section of the Tuileries Palace, the emperor would be able to see two arches: the first, which was being built in the Place du Carrousel, would serve as the main entrance to the Tuileries courtyard. The second, at the top of the Champs-Élysées, would crown the monumental vista dreamt up by the Bourbons and celebrate imperial glory.

In the footsteps of André Le Nôtre

Sketched out under Henri IV, the opening going from the heart of the Tuileries had been laid out under Louis XIV by the landscape architect André Le Nôtre, at the request of Jean-Baptiste Colbert. Planted with trees in staggered rows, the Grand Cours became the Champs-Élysées at that time. At the top, the hill of Chaillot was still muddy countryside outside Paris and crisscrossed with bad roads. As it was located on the path of the king when he hunted in the Bois de Boulogne, Le Nôtre designed an octagonal square of about 100 metres in diameter, planted with two rows of trees, there. Parisians immediately dubbed this new place for strolling the "*butte de l'Étoile*".

Over the reigns of various kings, the site would change without taking on its definitive design. As a result, soon after the French Revolution, it still had not been laid out. Napoleon's decision to erect a triumphal arch there thus came just at the right moment.

General indifference

Champagny confided the realisation of the monument to the architect Jean-François Chalgrin, assisted by his colleague

Jean-Arnaud Raymond. It got off to a bad start: the two men did not get along and presented different projects to the emperor. The former was inspired by Antiquity, the latter by the Italian Renaissance. Chalgrin envisaged an arch decorated with four freestanding Corinthian columns, his rival envisaged engaged columns.

In addition to these differences, bad luck plagued the project: for some obscure reason, the imperial decree of 18 February 1806, the monument's true birth certificate, was not recorded or published in *Le Moniteur*. Officially, it did not exist.

As for the laying of the first stone, planned for 15 August 1806, Napoleon's birthday, it took place without any official ceremony and to general indifference. That day, the emperor accepted the tribute of the ambassadors in Saint-Cloud. Moreover, the stone only exists because of the will of the workers. Placed on the foundations, in the centre, between the two pillars of the small arch overlooking Avenue Kléber, it bears the following inscription: "1806, fifteenth of August, birthday of His Majesty Napoleon the Great, this stone is the first that was laid on the foundation of this monument."

Laborious earthworks

Begun on 11 May 1806, the work on the foundations did not progress because of the porosity of the chalky soil. An underground platform, 54 metres long and 27 metres wide, had to be built to support the structure's mass. The earthworks were laborious. After a year, the foundations were only 6 metres deep. To make matters worse, the entrepreneur had great difficulty in obtaining stone and recruiting workers. The construction moved at a snail's pace.

On 3 March 1808, Pierre-François-Léonard Fontaine, first architect to the emperor, pronounced himself in favour of a single arch and deemed columns unnecessary. He also explained that "in such a high location, it was absolutely essential that it be colossal in size" (Jean Tulard, *Dictionnaire Napoléon*, vol. I, 109). That is how Chalgrin's working drawing prevailed over the plans of Raymond, who threw in the towel. Although the Arch of Titus in Rome, with a single opening,

served as a model for Chalgrin, he had to pierce the side elevations in order to allow traffic to circulate.

For the structure, the white stone of L'Isle-Adam, which had been chosen at the start, was abandoned in favour of the harder stone of Château-Landon, near Nemours. A new quarry thus had to be opened, which slowed the works down even further.

The foundations were barely at ground level when Chalgrin's plans were finally accepted on 27 March 1809. The estimate was for 9,132,000 francs, a huge sum at the time.

In front of each of its piers, the arch was to be decorated with pedestals topped with trophies and adorned with bas-reliefs; an eagle was to be sculpted in the centre of the main vault, in the middle of the coffer and rosettes. Inside, the architect envisaged a huge vaulted room above the main arch, as well as empty spaces. On the Paris side, they were to contain spiral stairs and on the Neuilly side, downpipes. The structure was to be crowned with a platform surrounded by a Corinthian cornice, intended to contain a group of sculptures.

A life-size model

Chalgrin's efforts were far from over. The Arc du Carrousel had been finished for a year while his arch was still just 6 metres high. Over seventy years of age, the architect was losing hope of ever seeing his work finished.

An unexpected event raised his spirits: Napoleon's upcoming marriage. Having divorced Josephine, Napoleon was preparing to wed the daughter of the emperor of Austria, the archduchess Marie-Louise. The ceremonies were planned for the first two days of April 1810. After the civil marriage in Saint-Cloud, the sovereigns would make their entrance into Paris and go to the Louvre for the religious ceremony.

This was a godsend for Chalgrin, who proposed to put up—on the pillars under construction—a wooden framework covered with painted canvases representing the finished monument.

The emperor approved of the idea and 500 workers were immediately hired to build a 45-metre-high wooden frame.

But the task was difficult during the late winter of 1810. Sudden downpours, gusts of wind, and accidents threatened

The end of the Empire and of construction

Beginning in 1812, the reduction in the funds earmarked for the arch's construction caused the works to slow down once again. Napoleon explained that the preparations for the war against Russia were the priority: "The Arc de Triomphe, Pont d'Iéna, and Temple de la Gloire can all be delayed two or three years without objections" (*Souvenir napoléonien*, 432 [January 2001], 45). Despite the bad news, the disastrous retreat from Russia, and the defeats of the German campaign, Goust finished the construction and the decoration of the small side arches. When Napoleon abdicated in April 1814, the monument stood about 20 metres high: that is, as high as the impost of the main arch.

Napoleon left for the island of Elba. In the wake of the allied troops, Louis XVIII entered Paris on 2 May 1814, which brought the building works to an immediate halt. The following year, Napoleon's brief return did not allow for a resumption of works and the defeat at Waterloo sounded the knell of the First Empire.

After the scaffolding was taken down, the arch's four pillars soon began to look like ancient ruins. One of them served as a look-out post for the defenders of Paris. The wood from the project was used to cover the vast granaries recently built near the Arsenal, as well as to construct the studio of François Bosio, who was working on the statue of Louis XIV for Place des Victoires.

An awkward legacy

Unlike his brother, the future Charles X, Louis XVIII was not a king who liked to build. He contented himself with concealing the scars of the Revolution on public buildings, while taking over some of the emperor's projects, which he had covered in fleurs-de-lis. But the Arc de Triomphe was a source of worry to him because of its immense size and, above all, the extent of the works that remained to be carried out. The architect Guillaume Poyet suggested that he have it razed to the ground; the engineer Louis Bruyère, director general of the Travaux Publics de Paris, suggested that it be transformed into a water

Entrance of Their Majesties Napoleon I and Marie-Louise, anonymous, engraving (Paris, Musée Carnavalet).

the architect's gamble on several occasions. And the workers got involved: the carpenters instigated two strikes to demand pay rises, which they obtained. The chief of police broke the third strike by arresting the six ringleaders.

Meanwhile, in his studio in Rue de Tournon, the painter Louis Lafitte and his colleagues put the finishing touches on the decorations and bas-reliefs painted in *trompe-l'oeil* on the canvases.

In total, it took twenty days to put up the imitation triumphal arch that Napoleon and Marie-Louise's coach crossed to great cheering from Parisians on 1 April 1810. That evening, the real star of the show, it sparkled under Chinese lanterns and Bengal lights.

The life-size model of his arch allowed Chalgrin to spot its defects. But he had barely had the modifications ratified, notably the removal of the pedestals on the sides, when he died on 20 January 1811, at the age of seventy-two. His pupil, Louis-Robert Goust, then inspector of works, took on the project. Appointed architect of the structure on 1 May 1811, he scrupulously carried on the work of his master.

tower supplied by the Bassin de la Villette. The water would gush forth into basins placed along the Champs-Élysées.

The king was hesitant, but, on 9 October 1823, he signed an edict confirming the completion of the triumphal arch.

To the surprise of Parisians, who thought that the project had been abandoned for good, works recommenced during the autumn of 1823. Only the monument's dedication changed: *exeunt* the Empire and Napoleon's armies. The Bourbons were in charge again to celebrate the victories of the Spanish expedition, led by the Duc d'Angoulême, son of the future Charles X and nephew of the king. Victor Hugo approved of the decision:

> You whose distant curve the golden sunset
> Fills with celestial azure, enormous arch.
> ("À l'Arc de Triomphe", *Les Voix intérieures*)

> Raise yourself to the heavens, portico of victory!
> So that the giant that is our glory
> May pass without stooping!
> ("À l'Arc de Triomphe de l'Étoile",
> *Odes et Ballades,* Book II, eighth ode)

Goust was still the monument's architect, but he had to share his title with Jean-Nicolas Huyot. It was the beginning of a new duel: the two men had diametrically opposed conceptions of architecture, which slowed down the progress of the works. Moreover, the Conseil des Bâtiments Civils harshly criticised Chalgrin's plan, particularly the recessing of the main arch. It commissioned Huyot to modify the original plans.

Greatly inspired by the architecture of Ancient Rome, Huyot hoped to restore the columns and pedestals denied Chalgrin. For the upper part of the arch, he devised thirty-six statues symbolising the principal cities of France.

The umpteenth start

Charles X, who had just succeeded his brother Louis XVIII, decided that the initial project was to be respected, as the modifications entailed reworking the foundations, a risky and costly undertaking. This was a stroke of bad luck for Huyot, who had begun the transformations without obtaining permission from the government. This resulted in his dismissal on 16 December 1825.

A commission was immediately set up to oversee the reprised works orchestrated by Goust. Headed by Guy de Gisors, it was made up of Fontaine, Éloi Labarre, and François Debret, as Charles Percier refused to participate. It chose the ornamentation of the principal vault—twenty-one caissons and rosettes—and decided that all of the arch's decoration be executed in stone from Chérence, in the Vexin region, which was easier to quarry and transport than that of Château-Landon.

In January 1828, taking advantage of the resignation of the prime minister, the Comte de Villèle, Huyot took up his post once again alongside Goust and was obliged to respect the existing structures. He built the cross-ribbed vault intended to support the upper paving, the entablature or upper section of the monument with its cornice of lions' heads. The sculptures for the spandrels of the main arch were commissioned from James Pradier. In 1829 Huyot placed in the keystone of the main arch, on the Champs-Élysées side, a plaque bearing an inscription in praise of his patrons and his own genius:

> THIS MONUMENT COMMENCED IN 1806 AND LONG INTERRUPTED, CONTINUED IN 1823, DURING THE REIGN OF LOUIS XVIII, KING OF FRANCE AND NAVARRE, IS TO THE GLORY OF LOUIS ANTOINE, DAUPHIN, CONQUEROR AND PEACEMAKER OF SPAIN.
> THE VICOMTE DE MARTIGNAC, MINISTER OF THE INTERIOR,
> THE VICOMTE SIMÉON, MEMBER OF THE COUNCIL OF STATE, DIRECTOR OF ARTS AND SCIENCES,
> THE VICOMTE HÉRICART DE THURY, MEMBER OF THE COUNCIL OF STATE, DIRECTOR OF PUBLIC WORKS, BY J. N. HUYOT, ARCHITECT OF THE MONUMENT.

In 1830 the architect commissioned the large models immortalising Charles X receiving the army corps, as well as the Duc d'Angoulême receiving the municipal authorities.

A few months later, three days of bloody revolutionary riots—the Trois Glorieuses—brought a brutal end to the reign of Charles X and the architectural dreams of Huyot.

Saved by Louis-Philippe

In reality, the Revolution of 1830 had a positive effect on the Arc de Triomphe. Proclaimed king of the French with the blessing of the barricades, Louis-Philippe sought legitimacy by reviving the past. He thus restored the arch's initial vocation. The only difference was that the monument was dedicated not only to Napoleon's victories, but also to all of the French armies of 1789 to 1815. The new king had not forgotten his own involvement in the battles of Valmy and Jemmapes.

On 31 July 1832, Guillaume-Abel Blouet took over from Huyot, dismissed once again, this time for mismanagement. The new architect's mission was to finish the monument by constructing the attic, large vaulted room (future museum), and acroterion with its balustrade, a real plinth destined to receive a crown.

While he was finishing the paving at the foot of the structure, Blouet proposed to decorate the vaulted room with paintings representing France distributing wreaths to the victors. The Italian painter Cesare Carnevali had already executed some of the frescos, when Adolphe Thiers ordered a halt to the work, preferring ordinary lime plaster instead. Today, visitors can see a small trace of a fresco, which was brought to light a few years ago by restorers.

Jobs for artists

Passionate about art, a collector and critic when the fancy took him, Thiers, then minister of the interior, had a finance act for major projects adopted by parliament. Voted on 27 June 1833, it allowed him to finish the Parisian projects begun during previous reigns. For the Arc de Triomphe, all the allegorical and historical decoration remained to be done, but all the sculptures conceived during the Restoration had to be rethought as their political signification had changed.

Thiers himself commissioned the sculptures. In agreement with Louis-Philippe, he retained the symbolic military events of the Revolution, Consulate, and Empire that were strong enough to bring together the nation around the idea of homeland: *The Departure of the Volunteers of 1792* was commissioned from François Rude, *The Triumph of 1810* from Jean-Pierre Cortot, and *Resistance* (1814) and *Peace* (1815) from Antoine Etex. For the bas-reliefs, two episodes of the revolutionary armies with *The Battle of Jemmapes*, in which the Duc de Chartres took part; *The Funeral of General Marceau*; three of General Bonaparte victories: *Crossing the Arcole Bridge*, *The Battle of Aboukir*, and *The Conquest of Alexandria*; and *The Battle of Austerlitz*, the monument's *raison d'être*.

The frieze surrounding the top of the Arc de Triomphe illustrates—between two allegories of France—*The Departure of the Armies* and *The Return of the Armies*. In perfect symmetry, this immense march-past of troops comprises a long central scene in praise of the nation on both main façades. The choice of sculptors also needed to reflect the national spirit of the monument, which explains the presence of artists belonging to the Classical school, such Cortot, Henri Lemaire, and Gabriel-Bernard Seurre, known as Seurre the Elder, and sculptors close to the new Romantic movement, such as Jean-Jacques Feuchère, Etex, Théodore Gechter, Charles Marochetti, and John-Étienne Chaponnière. No to mention the two celebrities: Pradier and Rude.

Twenty-two artists were working on the Arc de Triomphe at the time—a fact criticised by the monument's detractors, who deplored its lack of aesthetic homogeneity. But Louis-Philippe had wanted it to be both a "social" project, in order to give work to several sculptors, and an illustrated encyclopaedia of the various artistic movements of the era.

Three short-lived compositions

During a visit to the site on 27 April 1834, Thiers, filled with enthusiasm for the majesty of the structure, decided to top it with a monumental sculpture. This was quite a gamble as the statuary had to be in proportion with the exceptional dimensions of the arch to be visible from all sides, from near and far. Over a hundred projects as original as they were eccentric attempted to fulfil the minister's wishes. The greatest artists of the period, notably Pradier and Antoine-Louis Barye, looked into the theme of the symbolic eagle; others found inspiration in the quadriga of the Arc du Carrousel.

Only three projects got off the drawing board. In 1838, for the anniversary of the Trois Glorieuses, Seurre produced an ensemble in wood, plaster, and canvas painted with a *France Triumphant* driving a chariot drawn by six horses. Two years later, Blouet replaced it with his own composition in praise of the emperor in time for the return of Napoleon's ashes.

Much later, during the Third Republic, Alexandre Falguière executed *The Triumph of the Revolution* for the celebrations of 14 July 1882. The work was supposed to symbolise the Republic on a chariot drawn by rearing horses preparing to crush Anarchy and Tyranny, while Justice and Liberty attempt to hold them back. This life-size plaster group, perched upon the Arc de Triomphe, remained there for four years before bad weather got the better of its flimsiness.

The Arc de Triomphe had many other surprises in store for Thiers. In 1835, at the end of construction, when he was preparing to pay the contractors and artists, the Council of State asked him for the decree of 18 February 1806. Without the monument's founding act, he had no credit at his disposal. The document could not be found because it never existed. Accustomed to political pitfalls, the minister got round this difficulty by obtaining a certified copy of the decree from his counterpart at the Ministry of Justice. The Council of State was obliged to release the funds.

Unveiled on the quiet

All that remained to do was set the date for the unveiling. It took place on 29 July 1836, on the sixth anniversary of the Revolution of 1830, but in particularly disconcerting circumstances.

That day, at seven o'clock in the morning, Thiers, by then prime minister, was brought to the foot of the Arc de Triomphe in the company of his finance minister, the Comte d'Argout. The Place de l'Étoile was empty except for two official visitors, six National Guards, and the warden who had just greeted them and was dressed for the occasion in his old chief marshal of lodgings of the Dragoons uniform.

The monument was decorated with flags and wrapped in curtains to conceal the sculptures. The prime minister went round

the monument and conscientiously unveiled the works of the sculptors. After a final salute, Thiers and Argout went back to their offices.

In fact, the planned festivities were cancelled because the king feared assassination attempts. On 25 June 1836, Louis-Philippe was shot by the young Louis Alibaud. Since the attempt on his life by Giuseppe Fieschi that left eighteen dead and fifty wounded on 28 July 1835, the king no longer walked about in Paris. In addition to the king's fears, there was a question of diplomacy: he did not want to offend foreign chancelleries by celebrating with great pomp the battles in which they were defeated.

Silent on the failed ceremony, the press consoled itself by praising the illumination of the Arc de Triomphe, which, like an enormous diamond, sparkled with a thousand gaslights in the night that followed the strangely subdued unveiling.

The following day, it was Parisians' turn to discover the monument. An enthusiastic Victor Hugo dedicated a few verses to it in *Les Voix intérieures* and *Odes et Ballades*:

This cross section of the monument's north-south axis allows us to situate the vaulted room designed by the architect Guillaume-Abel Blouet, watercolour and gouache drawing by Jules-Denis Thierry (Paris, BHVP).

ORNEMENTS DE L'IMPOSTE DV GRAND ARC. BASE DV MONVMENT. IMPOSTE ET ARCHIVOLTE DES PETITS ARCS. PETITES VOVTES. DECORATION SOVS LE GRAND ARC.

Details of the decoration of the impost of the main arch, watercolour and gouache drawing by Jules-Denis Thierry (Paris, BHVP).

O vast pile carved by history!
Pile of stone sitting on a pile of glory!
Extraordinary edifice!
("À l'Arc de Triomphe",
Les Voix intérieures)

Triumphal arch! lightning, by laying low your master,
Seemed to have struck your yet to be born front.
Through our new exploits here you stand again!
For we did not want, for our illustrious army,
That it be an unfinished monument
To our renown!
("À l'Arc de Triomphe de l'Étoile",
Odes et Ballades, book II, eighth ode)

The battle of the inscriptions

The first visitors were surprised at the inscriptions. The wishes of Napoleon I, who wanted to see the names of the marshals, generals, and colonels who had fought under him during the glorious campaign of 1805 represented, were not respected.

To mask the bareness of the inner pillars, the architect Blouet suggested carving the names of the great victories and heroes of 1792 to 1815. Swayed by the proposition, Thiers asked General Cyr-Nugues, known as "Baron Saint-Cyr-Nugues", field officer during the Spanish campaign, to draw up a list of battles and officers to be honoured. Thus, from Valmy to Ligny, ninety-six battles figured over the thirty shields of the attic and the inner faces of the piers supporting the arches. The 384 selected heroes occupied the walls located under the small vaults.

It resulted in an incredible storm of protest. Some were outraged to see the name of Turreau, the "butcher" of the Vendée, others deplored the absence of François-Christophe Kellermann, Louis-Charles Desaix, and Jean-Victor Moreau. As for Victor Hugo, he was upset not to see the name of his father, General Hugo, who had won fame during the Spanish campaign. His disappointment was voiced in two verses in *Les Voix intérieures* (from the poem "À l'Arc de Triomphe"):

I regret nothing before your sublime wall
But absent Phidias and my forgotten father!

Most of the complaints obtained satisfaction. The unlucky Blouet, the unwitting guilty party, was tearing his hair out: he had to find room for the names of another 70 battles and 233 names. He barely managed to when seven names were added in 1841 and twelve in 1842. And it was far from settled. Louis and Jérôme Bonaparte, for example, would have to wait until their son and nephew Napoleon III came to power in 1850 to figure on the Arc de Triomphe. From 1851 to 1895, sixteen additional demands were met. This brought the total to 697 names and 174 battles.

On the inner faces of the Arc de Triomphe are inscribed the names of battles and sieges won. Between each group of names, the French cockerel, encircled by an oak wreath, alternates harmoniously with the imperial eagle encircled by a laurel wreath, drawing by Jules-Denis Thierry (Paris, BHVP).

The mark of the Second Empire

In the 1840s, the Place de l'Étoile was yet to be laid out and the Arc de Triomphe emerged from a moonlike setting where rubble, hillocks, and stony scree got in the way of those strolling. The *place* only changed appearance during the Second Empire, thanks to the policy of major improvements to Paris undertaken by the prefect of the Seine *département*, Georges-Eugène Haussmann.

In 1854 Napoleon III approved the plans of a Cologne-born architect, Jacques-Ignace Hittorff, who had already transformed Place de la Concorde and the Champs-Élysées. Inspired by the roundabout marked out by Le Nôtre in the past, the architect designed a round *place* 240 metres in diameter, with 12 avenues laid out in a star pattern and intersected by a circular road. This arrangement allowed for twelve town houses to be built. The height of their façades was restricted to 16 metres by Hittorff, so as not to overwhelm the Arc de Triomphe. Finding that these buildings, know as "des Maréchaux" were too low given the size of the *place*, Haussmann ordered that a triple row of trees be planted to hide them. Napoleon III did not agree and took the architect's side. And Haussmann immediately rallied round the emperor! Not afraid of going back on his decision, he even wrote in his memoirs: "I consider this beautiful layout, which I am proud of having been able to find, as one of the greatest successes of my administration." A master of the art of rewriting history.

The Arc de Triomphe as it appeared around 1840. The two pavilions by Ledoux were not demolished until 1861, when the *place* was laid out.

Napoleon under his arch

On 5 May 1821, Napoleon died in Saint Helena without having seen his arch finished. But the emperor's remains passed underneath it on 15 December 1840, during the return of the ashes decreed by Louis-Philippe. In "The Emperor's Return" (*Poems in Three Volumes*, vol. 1, Boston: n.d.), Hugo had predicted:

Sire, to thy capital thou shalt come back,
Without the battle's tocsin and wild stir;
Beneath the arch, drawn by eight steeds coal black,
Dressed like an emperor.

Despite the fact that it was freezing cold, a huge crowd jostled along the route taken by the cortège from the Avenue de Neuilly (now Avenue de la Grande-Armée) to the Hôtel des Invalides. Sixteen black horses, harnessed to quadrigae, drew the funeral carriage draped with crape carrying the catafalque. The architect Henri Labrouste had designed a sort of multi-storey golden mausoleum atop four golden wheels. Fourteen caryatids representing the victories of Napoleon supported the coffin, which was covered with the imperial mantle, upon which were placed sword, crown, and sceptre. The whole weighed 13 tonnes and measured 10 metres high.
Hundreds of men accompanied the convoy, which advanced slowly between the lines of columns topped with imperial eagles, as well as with burning torches and statues depicting the great figures of French history.
While batteries fired several salutes, the carriage stopped underneath the Arc de Triomphe, decorated for the occasion by Abel Blouet. In *Choses vues* (Paris: Gallimard, 2002, 110), Hugo, a critical onlooker, did not mince words when it came to the architect's work: "A mediocre opera set occupies the top of the Arc de Triomphe, the emperor standing on a chariot surrounded by figures of renown, with Glory to his right and Grandeur to his left. What does a statue of grandeur signify? How can grandeur be expressed by a statue? This is utter twaddle. This badly gilt decoration looks over Paris. Walking round the arch, one can see it from behind. It is a real stage farm. On the Neuilly side, the emperor, the Glories, and the Fames are but roughly scribed frames."

Then the carriage continued along its route towards the Invalides to cries of "Long live the Emperor!" Hugo lingered at Place de l'Étoile. He saw the horses of the imperial harness return: "At about five o'clock, the carriage-catafalque, now empty, came back along the Avenue des Champs-Élysées in order to take cover under the arch of the Étoile. This was a lovely idea" (Victor Hugo, *Choses vues*, op. cit., 111).

The heart of the nation

It took the Arc de Triomphe several decades to enter into the consciousness of Parisians. But by the late 1840s, it had become the heart of the nation. It now beat in time with the major events in French history.
That was the case on 20 April 1848, for the Fête de la Fraternité (Festival of Brotherhood) when the provisional government, presided by physicist François Arago, distributed the flags of the new republic to the army and National Guard.
Four years later on 2 December 1852, when the Second Empire was proclaimed, Napoleon III passed underneath the arch to make his entrance into Paris.
In 1871 the monument also experienced the darkest hours of the Franco-Prussian War. On 1 March, the victorious Prussian

Return of the Ashes of Napoleon I on 15 December 1840, drawing, French school, 19th century (Versailles, Châteaux de Versailles).

Communards hoisted a battery of cannons onto its platform. More than fifty shells were fired on 10 April 1871 alone, causing the whole structure to vibrate so much that it frightened the insurgents. They stopped firing and turned it into a look-out post. During the siege, the groups sculpted by Etex on the west façade were hit by shrapnel.

To Victor Hugo

On 1 June 1885, France held a state funeral for Victor Hugo. For one night and one day, the great man's remains lay in state under the Arc de Triomphe in a catafalque 22 metres high designed by Charles Garnier, the architect of the Opéra. At the top, large silver teardrops surrounded the deceased's initials. An immense crape veil, departing from Falguière's group, which was still in place, draped the left side of the monument. On the lighting columns bearing the flags at half-mast, escutcheons displayed the titles of Hugo's works of literature. Underneath the small arches, "France to Victor Hugo" could be read on very large medallions

After the customary speeches in the presence of the senior branches of the civil service, the huge cortège left the Arc de Triomphe for the Pantheon. Two million people attended the magnificent ceremony.

14 July 1919

It was not until the end of World War I and the victory parade on 14 July 1919 that there was such an impressive crowd around the Arc de Triomphe again.

The man behind the event, Georges Clemenceau, had an immense gilt cenotaph placed under the main arch in homage to the 1.5 million dead combatants. The work of Gustave Jaulmes, Louis Sue, and André Mare, the monument, which weighed 30 tonnes and was 17 metres high, was decorated with Victories, aeroplane wings, and lictors' fasces on its four sides. In enormous letters was the inscription: "To those who died for France." At the last minute, Clemenceau decided to move the cenotaph to enable troops to pass under the arch. Nearly a

troops entering Paris had to skirt round it. The Arc de Triomphe was fenced off by a rubble barricade put up by a population prepared to do battle if the Prussians dared violate the symbol of the nation. Later, after the departure of the occupying forces, Parisians purified the premises by burning the wooden frames protecting the sculptures.

In 1871 the riots of the Paris Commune did more damage to the Arc de Triomphe than the war and enemy bombardments, which it had escaped unscathed. During the siege of Paris, the

France honours its heroes

On 14 July 1919, when the ceremony was over, an anonymous crowd, made up mainly of mothers and widows, surrounded the Arc de Triomphe and kneeled to pray in front of the cenotaph. In impressive silence, at the foot of the monument dedicated by Napoleon to his soldiers, the cult of those who died for their country was spontaneously created.

No one would forget it. On 11 November 1920, to honour the memory of soldiers killed in action during World War I, the Arc de Triomphe received the remains of the Unknown Soldier (see p. 67).

These events confirmed the vocation of the Arc de Triomphe. Since the return of Napoleon's ashes, it has been dedicated to the cult of heroes and historical memories. It saw the passage of the remains of Lazare Carnot, brought back from exile; Marshal Lyautey, repatriated in 1962 after the independence of Morocco; and President Sadi Carnot, assassinated in 1894 by an Italian anarchist; and the tributes to marshals Mac-Mahon, Foch, Joffre, Leclerc de Hautecloque, and de Lattre de Tassigny. Not forgetting the 1915 ceremony of the transfer of the ashes of Claude-Joseph Rouget de Lisle, author of "La Marseillaise", from the Choisy cemetery to the Invalides.

Victory celebrations at the Arc de Triomphe, 14 July 1919 (Paris, Musée de l'Armée).

Marshals Foch and Joffre leading the victory parade, 14 July 1919.

Burying the coffin of the Unknown Soldier underneath the Arc de Triomphe, 28 January 1921.

thousand disabled ex-servicemen marched past, while Marshal Joffre and Marshal Foch on horseback led the military parade. Behind them were the inter-Allied *état-major* followed by the American, British, Belgian, Italian, Greek, Polish, Czech, Serbian, Croatian, and Japanese detachments. The French army, led by Marshal Pétain on a white horse, brought up the rear. The immense crowd could barely contain its emotion when the standards of the regiments passed by, torn, dirty, testimony to horrible battles: Verdun, Douaumont, Argonne, Marne, and Somme. All the services were officially represented. Or nearly all, as aviation seems to have been forgotten. Furious, the pilots that had observed the parade from the Escadrille bar on the Champs-Élysées planned their revenge. In the early hours of 9 August, Charles Godefroy, at the controls of his biplane, avenged the affront by flying under the Arc de Triomphe at full speed. The flying ace did not know at the time that people would imitate him.

Every year on the French national holiday, 14 July, the Patrouille de France flies over the Arc de Triomphe and the Champs-Élysées.

Celebrations on 14 July 2006:
heir to the Paris municipal
guard founded by Bonaparte
during the Consulate,
the Republican Guard
parades in front of
the Arc de Triomphe
and is always warmly
applauded by the public.

Charles de Gaulle leaves his mark

On 14 June 1940, Parisians kept a low profile while Wehrmacht troops marched past the monument. France had lost the war, Nazi Germany was triumphant.

Four years later, on 25 August 1944, General Leclerc's Second Armoured Division liberated Paris. The following day, General de Gaulle, president of the Provisional Government of the French Republic, placed a spray of flowers in the shape of the cross of Lorraine on the Tomb of the Unknown Soldier before going down the Champs-Élysées amidst a vast crowd. "It looked more like the sea!" he wrote in his memoirs. "A tremendous crowd was jammed together on both sides of the road. Perhaps two million people. The roofs too were black with many more" (*War Memoirs: Unity, 1942–1944*, trans. Richard Howard, London: Weidenfeld and Nicolson, 1959, 311).

Charles de Gaulle seemed to link his destiny to Napoleon's monument. It was there that he received Winston Churchill on 11 November 1944 and John F. Kennedy in 1961. After the wild days of May 1968 that nearly brought down the Fifth Republic, de Gaulle took the situation in hand. On 30 May 1968, he announced, "I will not step down. . . . The Republic will not abdicate." The televised speech provoked a veritable "Gaullist landslide": a million people marched behind ministers Michel Debré and André Malraux, from Place de la Concorde to the Arc de Triomphe.

The last episode took place on 12 November 1970. Three days after his death, Charles de Gaulle was buried in Colombey-les-Deux-Églises and a requiem mass at Notre-Dame de Paris was attended by more than eighty heads of state. That evening, a vast and silent crowd walked up the Champs-Élysées to the Arc de Triomphe for a final tribute.

Given the popular acclaim, the Paris city council decided to rename the Place de l'Étoile after Charles de Gaulle a few days later.

The setting for celebrations

While the Arc de Triomphe remained a special "site of memory" for the French nation and an essential stop on state visits by foreign heads of state, it also has a role to play on public holidays. On the evening of 14 July 1989, it was one of the centrepieces of the multiethnic parade devised by Jean-Paul Goude to celebrate the bicentenary of the French Revolution. On 24 June 1990, a harvest festival saw it isolated in the middle of a huge wheatfield, given over to harvesters. On 12 July 1998, it was surrounded by a jubilant crowd that had come to celebrate the World Cup victory of the French national football team.

During the military parades of 14 July, the Arc de Triomphe plays a central but little-known role: every year for a few days, the monument becomes the most unusual control tower in the world. The air show is controlled from the platform, which is taken over by highly sophisticated equipment. This strategic role would not displease the victor of Austerlitz, Napoleon.

Liberation of Paris. General Charles de Gaulle at the Arc de Triomphe de l'Étoile, 26 August 1944.

Parade of tanks in front of the Arc de Triomphe during the 14 July 2006 celebrations.

Following pages

Aerial view of the Arc de Triomphe looking west towards La Défense and its Grande Arche along the Avenue de la Grande-Armée.

Aerial view of the Arc de Triomphe looking east towards the Jardin des Tuileries and the Musée du Louvre along the Avenue des Champs-Élysées.

Views of
the Arc de Triomphe

The lower pier reliefs

The Triumph of Napoleon
by Jean-Pierre Cortot
(1787–1843).
*Lower relief, south-east pier.
Facing Avenue
des Champs-Élysées.*
In Roman dress, Napoleon
holds a sword against his
chest while Victory crowns
him with a laurel wreath.
To the left, the emperor
extends a protective hand
over the allegory of a
conquered city, and Clio
inscribes on a tablet the
major events of his reign.
At the top, winged Fame
sounds a trumpet and bears
the imperial eagle. Cortot
produced a classical, soulless
composition to evoke the
zenith of Napoleon's reign.

The Departure of the Volunteers of 1792, known as La Marseillaise by François Rude (1784–1855). *Lower relief, north-east pier. Facing Avenue des Champs-Élysées.* A winged woman representing the spirit of war calls for volunteers while indicating the site of the battle with her sword. In the foreground, a bearded warrior in a coat of mail leads a naked young man by the shoulder. At the top left, a cockerel dominates the scene. Rude depicted the conscription of 1792 when 200,000 men set off to defend the country under the orders of the Legislative Assembly. The artist harmoniously combines classical tradition and the poetic universe of Ossian to produce an intensely Romantic work.

Peace by Antoine Etex
(1808–1888).
Lower relief, north-west pier.
Facing Avenue
de la Grande-Armée.
After the Treaty of Paris
of 1815, a France at peace
went back to work.
In the centre, a nude soldier
wearing a helmet puts his
sword back in its sheath.
On the left, a young boy
reads while his mother plays
with the baby on her lap.
On the right, a kneeling
peasant examines his
ploughshare. Behind them,
a labourer brings a bull under
control. Minerva, helmeted
and armed with her spear,
watches over them. Despite
the sumptuousness of
the sculptures, Etex's figures
do not come to life.

The Resistance
by Antoine Etex (1808–1888).
Lower relief, south-west pier.
Facing Avenue
de la Grande-Armée.
A standing nude young
warrior, left fist clenched,
holds a two-edged sword
in his other hand.
On the left, an old man tries
to hold him back;
on the right, a pleading
woman holds a dead child.
Behind him, a bearded
horseman falls from his
mount, symbolising the
patriot's sacrifice. At the top,
wings spread, the spirit
of the future brandishes
a flaming sword in his right
hand; his left fist is also
clenched as a sign
of resistance. Etex's
Romanticism inspired
this depiction of France's
resistance to
the invading Austrian
and Russian armies in 1814.

The upper pier reliefs

The Battle of Aboukir
by Gabriel-Bernard Seurre,
known as Seurre
the Elder (1795–1867).
Upper relief, south-east pier.
Facing Avenue
des Champs-Élysées.
On 25 July 1799, the British
landed in Aboukir Bay
with an Ottoman army
commanded by Mustapha
Pasha. With 10,000 infantry
and 1,000 horsemen under
the command of General
Murat, Napoleon launched
an offensive without waiting
for reinforcements from
General Kléber's division.
Murat seized the fort
and took Mustapha Pasha
prisoner while General

Lannes, who led two battalions,
seized the Ottoman redoubt.
The victory strengthened
the Armée d'Orient's
position, even though
Napoleon set off for France
a month later.
On the bas-relief, Seurre
depicted Napoleon
and Murat on horseback,
followed by French soldiers.
They advance towards the
prison camp where Mustapha
Pasha is under guard.
The generalissimo of the
Ottoman armies leans on his
young sons while a captive,
his forehead in the dust,
begs the victors for mercy.
Behind Bonaparte flies
the flag of the 22nd Brigade.

The Funeral of General Marceau by Henri Lemaire (1798–1880).
Upper relief, north-east pier. Facing Avenue des Champs-Élysées.

Defeated by General Kléber at Altenkirchen in June 1796, the Austrians took their revenge on 19 September, when Archduke Charles beat Comte Jourdan's army, which had to cross the Rhine. Major General Marceau, who was in command of the rear guard on the riverbank, was in charge of protecting the retreat of the French army. He died in battle at Altenkirchen on 21 September 1796, aged twenty-seven. François-Séverin Marceau-Desgraves, known as Marceau, did his recruit training in the Ancien Régime army before enlisting in the first battalion of volunteers of Eure-et-Loir in November 1791 and was lieutenant colonel when war was declared on Austria in March 1792.

He distinguished himself at the Battle of Fleurus with the Sambre-et-Meuse army, took Koblenz, and blockaded Mainz. Cut down in his prime, the young general with a bright future did not have the time to enter Napoleonic legend.

On Lemaire's bas-relief, Marceau's body, half-draped in his cloak, lies on a stretcher in the centre of the composition.

On the left, Archduke Charles, followed by four Austrian officers, places a wreath on the French general's remains.

On the right, the soldiers of the Sambre-et-Meuse army keep vigil over their leader. The soldier holding a horse by its bridle gazes at Marceau's face while an officer weeps on the chest of a soldier who is also in tears. In the centre of the composition, the wall of the house reads ALTENKIRKEN XXI SEPTEMBER 1796. At the very left of the sculpture is the signature, H. LEMAIRE, 1834.

Neither the Battle of Altenkirchen, which was more of a defeat, nor the death of General Marceau were themes chosen by Napoleon. It was Louis-Philippe who wanted to pay tribute to the young victims of the Revolution.

The Conquest of Alexandria by John-Étienne Chaponnière (1801–1835). *Upper relief, north-west pier. Facing Avenue de la Grande-Armée.* After having landed in Egypt in the cove of Marabout, Napoleon launched, after a night march of 13 kilometres, four thousand Armée d'Orient soldiers against the fortifications of Alexandria. On 3 July 1798, General Menou took the "triangular fort" while General Kléber and General Louis André Bon controlled two of the entries. Fearing that the city would be destroyed, the sheikhs and worthies agreed to lay down their arms, and at noon, Bonaparte entered the city. In the centre of the bas-relief, Chaponnière depicted Jean-Baptiste Kléber leading his men on the ramparts of Alexandria. The general, who was wounded in the head during the attack, holds his right hand to his forehead and brandishes his sword in the direction of the enemy with the other. A grenadier pierces the chest of the Turk who shot his leader with his bayonet, but does not see the nude Egyptian getting ready to stab him. The flag of the Armée d'Orient stands out against the mêlée, a tangle of bodies and weapons. As a sign of defeat, the Mameluke standard lies at the foot of the rampart. Below, at the base of the battlements, is the artist's signature, J. E. CHAPONNIÈRE, 1835.

Crossing the Arcole Bridge
by Jean-Jacques Feuchère
(1807–1852).
Upper relief, south-west pier.
Facing Avenue
de la Grande-Armée.
A famous episode from
the Italian campaign, which
took place in the marshes
20 kilometres from Verona,
against the Austrian armies.
On 15 November 1796,
while the attack led by
General Augereau failed on
the Arcole Bridge, Napoleon
arrived on the scene and
seized the flag of the first

battalion of the 51st Half-
Brigade (the former
99th Half-Brigade), shouting:
"Follow your general!"
Leading Augereau's
grenadiers, he leapt onto
the bridge under a hail of
bullets and grapeshot, which
was decimating both soldiers
and officers. His aide de
camp, Jean-Baptiste Muiron,
shielded him with his body
before falling down dead.
The battle, which had
only just begun, lasted
three days before ending
in a French victory.

Feuchère's bas-relief was
inspired by the well-known
painting by Horace Vernet.
Napoleon, a sword in
his right hand, brandishes
a flag with his left hand.
While he attempts to cross
the wooden bridge,
Colonel Muiron, on the
ground, intervenes. Behind
Bonaparte, General
Augereau leads his men,
while in the foreground
the young drummer
André Étienne sounds
the charge.

The lateral upper reliefs

The Battle of Austerlitz
by Théodore Gechter
(1796–1844).
North lateral upper relief.
Facing Avenue de Wagram.
The victory of 2 December
1805, which brought
the German campaign
to an end, was no ordinary
battle, as Napoleon
pretended to fear
the confrontation while
concealing the concentration
of his men; better still,
he laid a trap for the allies
by abandoning the Pratzen
Plateau to them. Hearing
the Austrian troops
manoeuvre in the fog, he had
the plateau occupied by
the corps of Marshal Soult.
When the fog lifted,
he noticed that most of
the allied army was engaged
in the depression: it was
the signal for attack.
Russians and Austrians
were overwhelmed by
the French infantry.
On the bas-relief, Napoleon,
on horseback, occupies the
centre. Surrounded by the
Imperial Guard, he observes
the Frency infantry charge
the enemy. Dismounted,
General Friant makes his way
through with the help of a
rifle while the Russian and
Austrian cavalry move back
over the frozen ponds
of Satschan whose ice breaks
under the horses' hooves.
On a piece of ice is inscribed:
T. GECHTER, 1836.

The Battle of Jemmapes
by Charles Marochetti
(1805–1868).
South lateral upper relief.
Facing Avenue Kléber.
After the Battle of Valmy,
General Dumouriez prepared
to invade Belgium with
40,000 men. Marching
on Mons, he confronted
the Austrian army of the Duke
of Saxony-Teschen on
the heights of Jemmapes
on 6 November 1792.
The young and inexperienced
volunteers did not dare
attack the Austrians and
it took all the spirit of
Dumouriez and his generals
to lead them to battle.
One of them, the Duc
de Chartres—the future
Louis-Philippe—showed real
leadership qualities at
nineteen years of age.
Far from being a masterpiece
of strategy, the victory
became legendary because
it was the first success of
the new republic.
In the centre of Marochetti's
bas-relief, Dumouriez,
on horseback, brandishes his
hat as a rallying sign;
he is followed by his
brigadiers, Rosières, Ferrand,
Stennebosse, the Duc de
Chartres, and Bloisières.
Behind them, a wounded
General Drouet is helped by
a health officer while General
Thouvenot, seen from
the back, sabre and hat
raised skywards, leads his
men into combat.
On the right, in the
foreground of the battle,
an Austrian officer, his arm
in a sling, is taken prisoner.
On the rim of a wheel is
the artist's signature,
C. MAROCHETTI, 1834.

The spandrels of the main arches

Fames
by James Pradier (1790–1852).
Spandrels of the main arches.
Facing Avenue
des Champs-Élysées.
Nudes despite the drapery,
hair streaming in the wind
and wings spread,
the goddesses sound
trumpets while one holds an
oak wreath (left tympanum),
and the other a laurel wreath
(right tympanum). The figures
of Fame were inspired
by those of the Arch of Titus
in Rome, casts of which
had been taken.

Fames by James Pradier
(1790–1852).
Spandrels of the main arches.
Facing Avenue
de la Grande-Armée.
Nude like the others and also
inspired by the figures of
Fame on the Arch of Titus,
these goddesses brandish
a laurel wreath tied with
strips of cloth in one hand;
in the other hand, leaning
against her shoulder,
one holds a trumpet
(left tympanum), the other,
a palm leaf (right tympanum).

Spandrels of the minor arches

Two allegorical figures
by Théophile Bra (1797–1863).
North outer minor arch.
Facing Avenue de Wagram.
On the left tympanum,
a nude grenadier, behind
whom flies the French flag
topped with the imperial
eagle, holds in his right hand
a rifle at ease, and an oak
branch in his left hand.
A nude chasseur occupies
the right tympanum.
He holds his rifle against
his chest. His left arm follows
the shape of the vault,
and he, too, brandishes an
oak branch in his left hand.
On the keystone
of the arch a tablet bears
the inscription, INFANTRY.

Two allegorical figures
by Achille-Joseph-Étienne
Valois (1785–1862).
South outer minor arch.
Facing Avenue Kléber.
On the left tympanum,
a nude carabineer, seen from
the back, holds his guidon in
his left hand and brandishes
a sabre in his right. Objects
including stirrups, a bit,
a bugle, and a rifle decorate
the corners. On the right
tympanum, a nude lancer,
seen from the front, seizes
his sabre with his right hand
while holding in his left hand
a rifle upon whose
barrel rests a helmet.
In the background are spurs,
epaulettes, a cartridge pouch,
and so on. On the keystone
of the arch a tablet bears
the inscription, CAVALRY.

The entablature friezes

Line engravings from Jules Denis Thierry's *Arc de Triomphe de l'Étoile*, Paris, 1845.

← Avenue
Kléber

East frieze
The Departure of the Armies

Hussars and Sappers of the Engineers
by Georges Jacquot (1794–1874).
*East frieze, right section of the side elevation
and left section of the central motif.*

← Avenue
de Wagram

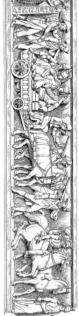

The Return of the Army from Egypt
by François Rude (1784–1855).
*West frieze, right section of the side elevation,
and left section of the central motif.*

Allegory
by Louis-Denis Caillouette (1790–1868).
West frieze, central section.

The friezes that encircle the 2.12-metre high Arc de Triomphe are 137 metres in length. Their sculptures were divided amongst six artists who were all allotted an equal surface area.

Avenue de Wagram →

Great Figures of the Revolution and the Empire
by Sylvestre Brun (1792–1855).
East frieze, central section.

Cavalrymen and Grenadiers
by Charles-René Laitié (1782–1862).
East frieze, right section of the central motif and left section of the side elevation.

West frieze
The Return of the Armies

Avenue Kléber →

The Return of the Army from Italy
by Gabriel-Bernard Seurre, known as Seurre the Elder (1795–1867).
West frieze, right section of the central motif and left section of the side elevation.

The Departure of the Armies

Frieze on the east entablature.
Facing Avenue des Champs-Élysées and half the lateral façades.

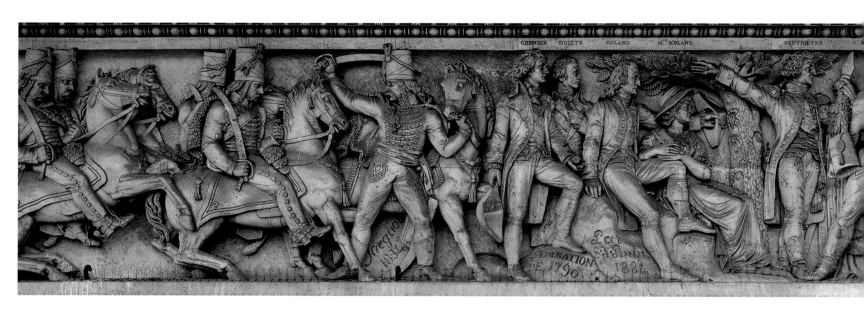

Great Figures of the Revolution and the Empire
by Sylvestre Brun
(1792–1855).
Central section.
The central section executed by Brun centres on the altar of the homeland, which bears the inscription, LAW | KING | COUNTRY.
On either side, the great figures of the era take flags in order to distribute them. Their names appear in a string course. These portraits were closely based on existing busts and period dress. Thus, we can see the smallpox scars on the Comte de Mirabeau's face and the deformed face of the painter Jacques-Louis

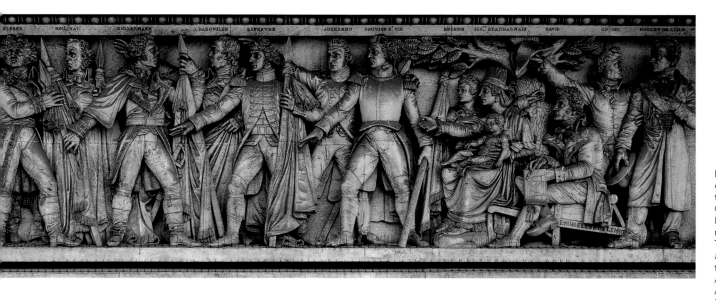

David who is drawing, seated on a wheelbarrow. To depict the uniform of Duc de Chartres, the future Louis-Philippe, the sculptor made use of his real uniform. The Duc d'Orléans, known as Philippe-Égalité, and the Duc de Bourbon wear Ancien Régime dress. Another sign of filial devotion, Louis-Philippe has not forgotten his maternal grandfather the Duc de Penthièvre, admiral of France, master of the hunt, and governor of Brittany, one of the rare princes of the royal blood not to have emigrated during the Revolution and who devoted the last years of his life to charity.

Great Figures of the Revolution and the Empire by Sylvestre Brun (1792–1855). *Details of the east entablature frieze.*
Two women are depicted in this work dedicated to the most important figures of the era: on the right, Josephine de Beauharnais holds her young daughter Hortense in her arms. She is sitting underneath a tree next to her son Eugène. On the left, Madame Roland is also sitting underneath a tree, her arm nonchalantly resting on Monsieur Roland's thigh. Josephine represents the link between the Ancien Régime, Empire, Restoration, and July Monarchy through the Revolution; she perfectly embodies the change in society. Her presence also pays tribute to Napoleon, the monument's unknown sponsor. Manon Roland, the Girondins' muse and a convinced revolutionary, who nevertheless ended up being guillotined. She made history by addressing these words to the Statue of Liberty while mounting the scaffold: "O Liberty, what crimes are committed in thy name!"

Top, from left to right

Cavalrymen and Grenadiers
by Charles-René Laitié
(1782–1862). *Right section
of the central motif.*
While Claude-Joseph Rouget
de Lisle, the author
de "La Marseillaise", is
the last in Joseph Brun's
gallery of figures, Laitié
depicts the cavalry followed
by the grenadiers with their
band and the soldiers
of Napoleon's old guard.

Cavalrymen and Grenadiers
by Charles-René Laitié
(1782–1862). *Left section
of the side elevation.*
On the north face
(Avenue de Wagram)
arrive the supply corps with
the wagons and caissons
of the artillery and Engineers.
The departure of the armies
begins and ends with
two winged spirits writing
down the names
of the departing soldiers.

Top, from left to right

Hussars and Sappers
of the Engineers
by Georges Jacquot
(1794–1874). *Right section*
of side elevation.
The south side (Avenue
Kléber) is dedicated
to the infantry. Soldiers guard
the baggage wagon while
a soldier puts on his gaiters
and another says his farewells
to his wife and child.

Bottom, from left to right

***Hussars and Sappers
of the Engineers***
by Georges Jacquot
(1794–1874). *Left section
of the central motif.*
A troop of hussars on
horseback, sabres in hand,
precedes the procession
of the infantry and the
musicians of the Imperial
Guard led by the drum major.

The Return of the Armies

Frieze on the west entablature.
Facing Avenue de la Grande-Armée and half the lateral façades.
This section of the frieze symbolises the entry into Paris of the victorious troops laden with trophies. To illustrate the rise of General Bonaparte, the artists depicted the conquests of Italy and Egypt.

Allegory
by Louis-Denis Caillouette
(1790–1868).
Central section.
Caillouette's contribution
begins and ends with
two triumphal arches.
In the centre, in front of
the inscription, To its brave
men, France is grateful,
an allegory of France
surrounded by Peace
and Plenty distributes laurel
wreaths to the fit
and wounded heroes who

lay trophies and flags taken
from the enemy at her feet.
Cavalrymen, grenadiers,
drummers, and infantrymen
converge towards the statue
of France; amongst them
is a soldier wearing a turban
and baggy trousers.
He evokes the many foreign
soldiers who came to fight
under the French flag,
such as the renowned
Mameluke Raza Roustam,
who remained in Napoleon's
service until 1814.

Allegory by Louis-Denis
Caillouette (1790–1868).
*Detail of the west
entablature frieze.*
Survivors and the wounded
congratulate each other
while one of their comrades
prepares to lay his trophies
at the feet of France.

Top, from left to right

**The Return of
the Army from Italy**
by Gabriel-Bernard Seurre,
known as Seurre the Elder
(1795–1867). *Right section
of the central motif.*
Welcomed by two townsmen
and two townswomen, a
group of soldiers get ready
to pass under a triumphal
arch bearing the inscription,
TO THE ARMÉE D'ITALIE. Then
comes a wagon harnessed to
four horses transporting
captured works of art,
including a classical statue
representing the Tiber, which
adorned the Villa Borghese
before entering the Louvre
on 9 November 1800.

Bottom, from left to right

**The Return of
the Army from Italy**
by Gabriel-Bernard Seurre,
known as Seurre the Elder
(1795–1867). *Left section
of the side elevation,
facing Avenue Kléber.*
Soldiers precede a wagon
drawn by oxen, containing
wounded soldiers and
an Italian woman holding
her child, who symbolises
Italy's submission to France.
The soldiers carry
sabretaches engraved with
the republican "R". Victory,
wings folded back, inscribes
the names of the victors.

Top, from left to right

**The Return of
the Army from Egypt**
by François Rude (1784–1855).
*Right section of the side
elevation, facing
Avenue de Wagram.*
A group of mounted
cavalrymen precedes
a horse-drawn wagon.
It transports the wounded,
including an Egyptian in
Mameluke dress who bears
witness to the clemency of
the French army. A winged
spirit in Egyptian clothing
and headdress inscribes
the heroic deeds of
the Egyptian expedition
in hieroglyphs.

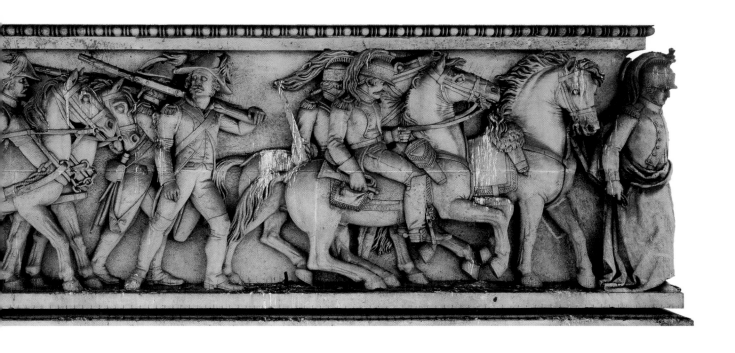

Bottom, from left to right

**The Return of
the Army from Egypt**
by François Rude (1784–1855).
*Left section of
the central motif.*
An enthusiastic crowd go
and meet the soldiers
of the Armée d'Égypte
who escort a statue
of a sphinx enthroned
on a cart yoked to four oxen.

Following pages

**The Return of
the Army from Egypt**
by François Rude (1784–1855).
*Right section of the side
elevation, facing
Avenue de Wagram.*

The inner spandrels

Two allegorical figures
by Joseph Debay (1779–1863).
Small south inner arch under the main vault. Facing Avenue de Wagram.
On the left tympanum, a nude and bearded soldier, his left foot resting on a cannonball, a civic crown in one hand, a flag in the other, symbolises heavy artillery. On the right tympanum, a nude young soldier embodies light artillery. In his right hand, he holds a plan and a compass; in his left hand, he holds his horse's bridle. On the keystone of the arch, a tablet bears the inscription, ARTILLERY.

Two allegorical figures
by Émile Seurre, known as Seurre the Younger (1798–1858).
Small north inner arch under the main vault. Facing Avenue Kléber.
On the left tympanum, a young man evokes the sailor surrounded by flags, sails, and naval instruments. On the right tympanum, a nude man, a baldric over his shoulder to represent the sailor, holds a palm. On the keystone of the arch, a tablet bears the inscription, NAVY.

The inner high reliefs

Right-hand page

The names of battles figure on the inner faces of the main arch's piers (right) while the names of generals, grouped together according to the geographic regions where their battles took place, occupy the inner pillars (left). The Eiffel Tower stands out between a pillar and a pier.

Victory over the South
by Antoine-François Gérard (1760–1843).
Inner high relief, south-west. Facing Avenue Kléber.
Seated in the centre, Victory holds in her right hand a sceptre topped with the imperial eagle and, in the other, a tablet upon which are inscribed the names of Bonaparte's great victories in Italy: Marengo, Rivoli, Arcole, and Lodi. On the left, two spirits make a trophy with captured arms. On the right, a sculptor spirit finishes a bust of Napoleon while another spirit places a wreath on the Emperor's forehead. On the pedestal supporting the bust, the spirit carves the imperial eagle topped with the initial of Napoleon I.

Victory over the West
by Jean-Joseph Espercieux (1757–1840).
Inner high relief, north-west. Facing Avenue Kléber.
Looking to the left, Victory extends her arms towards the military spirits over whom she holds laurel branches. Two spirits hold a garland of entwined fruit and flowers, a symbol of plenty.
To the left, a spirit presents Victory with a broken sceptre. Behind him, on a shield leaning against a quiver, are inscribed the names of the battles of Jemmapes and Fleurus. On the right, a spirit holds a broken diadem out to Victory. He leans against an anchor upon which we can read ESPERCIEUX 1830.

Victory over the North
by Astyanax-Scaevola Bosio (1793–1876).
Inner high relief, north-east. Facing Avenue de Wagram.
The Victory over the North, seated in the centre, has just inscribed the following on a tablet she holds in her left hand: Austerlitz, Jena, Friedland, Ulm, Wagram, and Eylau. She is still holding the stylus in her right hand. There is a wreath at her feet. Four spirits to her left and right, amongst various weapons, hold a garland whose ends spill over with fruit.

Victory over the East
by Joseph-Adolphe-Alexandre Walcher the Younger.
Inner high relief, south-east. Facing Avenue de Wagram.
Seated in the centre of the composition, Victory holds a palm in her right hand; her left hand rests on top of a marble tablet upon which are inscribed the names of the great Egyptian battles of Bonaparte: Alexandria, Pyramids, Aboukir, and Heliopolis. On the left, a spirit tries to drag off a second spirit who was just planted his flag in the ground, symbolising the taking possession of conquered provinces. Two the right, two standing spirits hold hands. One places a wreath on the head of the other. The East is symbolised by the Ottoman flags topped with a crescents, a crocodile in the foreground, and pyramids on the horizon.

BARBAN
DUR
MA
GAUTH
PELLE
MONTM
CA
DURR
WATH
SCHRA
VINCE
GENTIL
FOISSAC
LANA
LEJE

NAPLES

AUBRY
ROUSSEL D'H'
LEPIC
L'HERITIER
JACQUINOT
BOURCKE
DOMON
GIRARDIN
DARU
COEHORN
ROUSSEL
GIRARD...VIEUX
GUYOT
DAHLMANN
BRUN
ROMEUF
FRIEDERICHS

MANTOUE
TAGLIAMENTO
SEDIMAN
MONT THABOR
CHEBREISSE
BASSIGNANO
SAN GIULIANO
DIETIKON
MUTTA THAL
GENES

LE VAR
MONTEBELLO
LE MINCIO
CALDIERO
CASTEL FRANCO
RAGUSE
GAETE

The vaults

All the Arc de Triomphe's vaults are decorated with caissons featuring rosettes of acanthus leaves. Tori, or large curved mouldings, sculpted of laurel branches divide the caissons. Interlacing decorates the transverse arches separating the vaults.

Decorations of the entablature and the main vault. Watercolour and gouache drawing by Jules-Denis Thierry (Paris, BHVP).

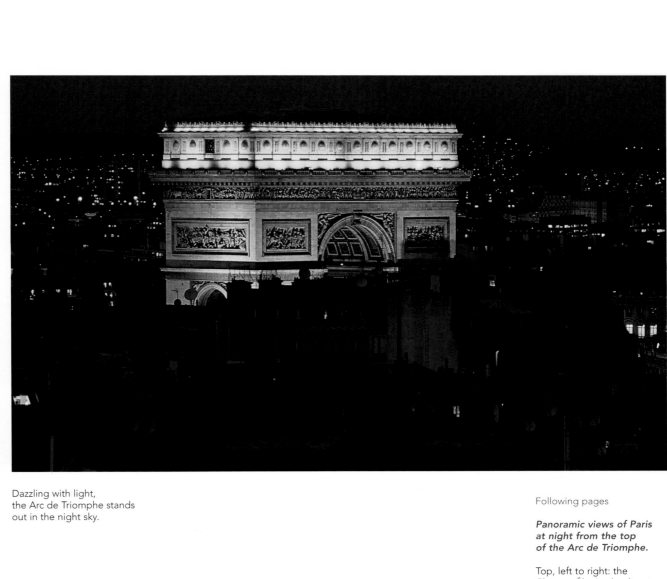

Dazzling with light,
the Arc de Triomphe stands
out in the night sky.

"You whose distant curve the golden sunset
Fills with celestial azure, enormous arch . . .
Your royal beauty is missing something.
The centuries will come for your apotheosis
And bring it to you."
(Victor Hugo, "À l'Arc de Triomphe",
Les Voix intérieures)

Following pages

***Panoramic views of Paris
at night from the top
of the Arc de Triomphe.***

Top, left to right: the
Champs-Élysées leading to
the illuminated big wheel,
which was the star attraction
of the millennium festivities,
with the towers of
Notre-Dame in the distance;
Avenue Marceau with the
dome of the Invalides and
the Montparnasse Tower in
the background; Avenue
Kléber and the Eiffel Tower.

Bottom, left to right: Avenue
Victor-Hugo, the more
imposing Avenue Foch,
Avenue de la Grande-
Armée—directly in line with
the Grande Arche de la
Défense—Avenue Carnot,
and Avenue Mac-Mahon.

In depth

A grateful France

The Unknown Soldier

Under the main vault of the Arc de Triomphe, an inscription carved into a grey stone slab attracts everyone's attention:

> HERE
> LIES
> A FRENCH
> SOLDIER
> WHO DIED
> FOR HIS COUNTRY
> 1914–1918.

The idea of putting the remains of a World War I combatant in the Pantheon dates to 1916. The project took shape and ended up being voted on by the Chamber of Deputies on 12 November 1919. But the war veterans thought that the choice of the Pantheon did not reflect the importance of the sacrifice. Thus, the writer and journalist Binet-Valmer began a campaign, relayed by the press, to bury the Unknown Soldier under the Arc de Triomphe. Thanks to the support of the prime minister, Georges Leygues, the deputies and senators both voted unanimously to pass the law of 8 November 1920, which stated that "the honours of the Pantheon would be paid to the remains of one of the unidentified soldiers who died for his country during World War I. The translation of the remains of the soldier was solemnly carried out on 11 November 1920. The same day, the remains of the Unknown Soldier were buried under the Arc de Triomphe". It was also decided to commemorate the fiftieth anniversary of the Third Republic and the memory of the statesman Léon Gambetta on the anniversary of the armistice.

Eight unidentified bodies of French soldiers were immediately taken from different parts of the front: Flanders, Artois, Somme, Île-de-France, Chemin des Dames, Champagne, Verdun, and Lorraine. The eight coffins, transported in one of the blockhouses of the Verdun citadel, were switched around several times.

During the afternoon of 10 November 1920, André Maginot, minister of pensions and president of the Fédération Nationale des Mutilés (National Federation of Disabled Ex-Servicemen), gave a bouquet of flowers gathered from the battlefield of Verdun to the youngest soldier in the 132nd Infantry Regiment, which made up the guard of honour in the chapel. The son of a combatant who died in action, Auguste Thin made history that day by placing the flowers on one of the coffins; with this gesture, he designated the Unknown Soldier. Brought to Paris that same evening, the coffin was placed in a chapel of rest erected at the foot of the *Lion of Belfort* on Place Denfert-Rochereau.

On the morning of 11 November, after a ceremony at the Pantheon, the carriage carrying Gambetta's heart and the gun carriage bearing the coffin of the Unknown Soldier draped with the French tricolour journeyed to the Arc de Triomphe. In front of an emotional crowd, the cortège advanced slowly, surrounded by a row of eight regimental flags of the Allied armies.

After this double tribute, the urn containing Gambetta's heart was returned to the Pantheon while the remains of the Unknown Soldier were placed in a room in the monument transformed into a chapel of rest. A guard watched over them day and night until they received a burial worthy of the symbol embodied: "Devotion, Abnegation, and Sacrifice".

The final inhumation took place on 28 January 1921, in the centre of the principal arch facing the Champs-Élysées, in the presence of President Alexandre Millerand and his cabinet. Eight non-commissioned officers decorated with the Médaille Militaire bore the coffin. Louis Barthou, then minister of war, placed the cushion to which were pinned the Légion d'Honneur, Médaille Militaire, and Croix de Guerre, "France's supreme tribute to the humble and anonymous heroes who died for her" on the flag covering him. All veterans' associations sent a delegation. Marshals Foch, Joffre, and Pétain attended the burial, as did David Lloyd George, the British prime minister. To the sounds of "La Marseillaise", the body was lowered into the tomb. From then on, a sacred tombstone covered the Unknown Soldier for eternity.

The memorial flame

Two years later, in an article published in *L'Intransigeant*, the journalist and poet Gabriel Boissy suggested extending the tribute to the Unknown Soldier with a flame: "A flame that represents the quivering, the presence of his soul; that burns like a permanent remembrance of every one of us, of the entire country."

The idea had the support of

Burial ceremony for the Unknown Soldier under the Arc de Triomphe, 28 January 1921.

Every day at 6.30 p.m., the memorial flame is rekindled during an unchanging ceremony.

Shield of the memorial flame, designed by the architect Henri Favier and executed by the ironworker Edgar Brandt.

André Maginot, then minister of war, and Léon Bérard, minister of education. Many projects were presented but it was that of the architect Henri Favier that won the competition. The ironworker Edgar Brandt produced the work that visitors still admire: at the head of the tomb, the flame rises from the muzzle of a cannon aimed at the sky; it is embedded in the centre of a reversed shield, whose chased surface depicts swords in a star pattern. On 11 November 1923, in the presence of General Henri Gouraud, military governor of Paris, and a multitude of veterans, Maginot lit the memorial flame for the first time.

For more than eighty years, the flame is relit every evening at 6.30 p.m. by representatives of various associations, according to an unchanging rite set by the commissioners of the association La Flamme sous l'Arc de Triomphe. Originally, only veterans' associations participated in the ceremony; now, as many of them have disappeared, the memorial flame committee has had to turn to other associations whose public-spiritedness is beyond reproach, such as the Red Cross and the Protection Civile.

Every day, two commissioners welcome the associations and oversee the ceremony. While the flame's special flag and its guard, and the bugle and the drum of the Republican Guard take position at the head of the tomb facing the Champs-Élysées, surrounded by standard bearers, the participants line up on either side of the tomb. At the drum roll, those present stand at attention while the delegations place their sprays of flowers on the tomb. Then the commissioner returns the bronze sword, which allows the president of the designated association to increase the height of the flame. The last post sounds and the flags are lowered for a minute of silence. When a military band is present, it plays "La Marseillaise" before the signing of the visitors' book. The ceremony ends with the "Hymn to the Unknown Soldier".

This rite has never been interrupted, even during the Occupation when about sixty volunteers met in turn under the Arc de Triomphe. There was no drum roll or last post but the rite was carried out and the minute of silence scrupulously observed. Germans who happened to be present at this moment moved respectfully away from the tomb and gave military salutes.

In August 1944, during the days preceding the liberation of Paris, the Germans' panic made the situation even more dangerous. Worried, the Comité de la Flamme decided that two guards should remain at the tomb day and night. Despite the danger, the associations continued to perform the rite, even on 25 August, during the arrival of Leclerc's tanks, when a German shell fired from Place de la Concorde exploded at the foot of Rude's *La Marseillaise*.

The Comité de la Flamme has decided to involve young people in the ceremony. According to the committee's president, General Jean Combette, who is concerned about the future, "It is a way of introducing them to their responsibilities as future citizens." While the Tomb of the Unknown Soldier still embodies the sacrifice of those who died on the battlefields and gave their lives for France, it has been enriched with a new symbol, that of "the faith in [France's] destiny". Rekindling the nation's flame is a way of looking to a future of peace and brotherhood.

From plates to gadgets

In 1815 the Arc de Triomphe was nothing but a building site but it had already caught the attention of earthenware makers. Montereau launched an initial series of plates whose central decoration depicted the Étoile tollgate and construction of the arch.

For the return of the ashes

In the early 1840s, the craze grew stronger. The Arc de Triomphe became a very popular item, closely associated with the emotion occasioned by the return of Napoleon's ashes. It was a godsend for the earthenware makers who produced several plates depicting various stages in the ceremony. One of the best known, manufactured by Creil in 1841, depicts the emperor's funerary carriage under the monument.

An official symbol

The image of the Arc de Triomphe began to symbolise Paris in the mid-1840s. And the Second Empire adopted it as part of its official decorum. In 1846, to immortalise the Paris visit of the viceroy of Egypt, Ibrahim Pasha, the artist Charles-Philippe Larivière painted the Arc de Triomphe in the background of his portrait.

On the occasion of the 1867 World's Fair, the Arc de Triomphe figured on many of the objects destined for the public. Not forgetting its conspicuous presence in the superb porcelain set of tableware, *Monuments de Paris*, produced by the Manufacture de Sèvres.

The period's most renowned painters showed an interest in

the Arc de Triomphe. Félix Ziem gave up the charms of Venice and the East for a while to depict the monument in an impressionistic manner.

Family matters

The Arc de Triomphe's majestic lines appealed to the entire family. They adorned women's powder boxes, decorated men's desk sets, and hid in puzzles for well-behaved children. Not to forget the Arc de Triomphe's participation in a French history-themed game of snakes and ladders that was very popular in the nineteenth century. The supreme privilege, the arch assured a player's victory.

Millions of postcards

The image of the Arc de Triomphe was also reproduced on millions of postcards, not to mention innumerable advertising, promotional, and tourist documents. But a rival overshadowed

Charles-Philippe Larivière, portrait of Ibrahim Pasha. The viceroy, wearing the sash and badge of the Grand Cross of the Légion d'Honneur awarded to him by Louis-Philippe, is portrayed in front of a view of the Arc de Triomphe. Oil on canvas, 1846 (Versailles, Châteaux de Versailles).

The Return of the Ashes. Napoleon's funeral procession enters Paris, 15 December 1840. China, Manufacture de Creil (Malmaison, Châteaux de Malmaison and Bois-Préau).

View of the triumphal arch erected at Place de l'Étoile. Porcelain, Manufacture de Creil et d'Aumale. Early 19th century (Malmaison, Châteaux de Malmaison and Bois-Préau).

it in this domain at the turn of the twentieth century: the brand new Eiffel Tower.

Fortunately, the Tomb of the Unknown Soldier gave the Arc de Triomphe a second wind beginning in 1920. The publication of postcards started up again with renewed vigour, as did the production of commemorative medals.

The monument's renewed popularity also allowed it to give its name to an internationally renowned horse race: the Prix de l'Arc de Triomphe. Created on 3 October 1920, it is still held every October at the Hippodrome de Longchamp.

A star stamp in 1944

In 1944 the Arc de Triomphe even became a star stamp. In anticipation of the Normandy landings, the Allied Military Government for Occupied Territories (AMGOT) decided to prepare a stamp for the soon-to-be liberated France. Produced in the United States, it depicts the Arc de Triomphe. Put into circulation for the first time in Carentan, Normandy, on 11 September 1944 it went into general use beginning on 9 October. The stamp's popularity and its brief period of use (about eight months) means that it is now highly coveted by stamp collectors.

View over the Champs-Élysées, taken from the Arc de Triomphe around 1840. Postcard, after engraving, c. 1900.

Panorama of the Arc de Triomphe de l'Étoile taken from a balloon. Postcard, c. 1900.

915. PARIS – Panorama de l'Arc de Triomphe de l'Étoile pris en ballon

H. Déposé

The architects of the Arc de Triomphe

Stamps depicting the Arc de Triomphe issued in the United States in 1944.

Unexpected roles

Although less dazzling than it was a century ago, the parallel career of the Arc de Triomphe is far from over. It continues to sell millions in the shape of pins, paperweights, snow globes, and various other gadgets every year.

And it sometimes takes on unexpected roles: on a label for cheese, transformed into an immense CD boxed set to house the 746 songs of the oeuvre of Charles Aznavour, or in stylised form as a brooch skilfully set with brilliant- and baguette-cut diamonds.

Jean-François Chalgrin (1739–1811)

A pupil of Étienne-Louis Boullée and Giovanni Nicolo Servandoni, Paris-born Chalgrin, who trained in Italy, entered the Académie d'Architecture in 1770. Architect to the king and the Comte de Provence, then *intendant des bâtiments* to the Comte d'Artois, he built private homes in Versailles and Paris, including the Hôtel de La Vrillière. He also built the church of Saint-Philippe-du-Roule, extended the Collège de France, and transformed the Palais du Luxembourg. Made a member of the Institut de France in 1799, he was commissioned to build the Arc de Triomphe in 1806. Even though the monument had barely gotten off the ground when he died, he is still considered its architect.

Jean-Arnaud Raymond (1742–1811)

The Toulouse native went to Paris to learn his craft with Jacques-François Blondel, author of the renowned *Cours d'architecture*. As he and Chalgrin did not see eye to eye on plans

for the Arc de Triomphe, he chose to resign. His architectural works are located in Montpellier and Nîmes.

Louis-Robert Goust (1761–?)

A native of the Ouche region, Chalgrin's pupil and collaborator

took part in the transformation of the Palais du Luxembourg. In 1819 he built the parish church of Beaumesnil, Eure, the village where he was born.

Jean-Nicolas Huyot (1780–1840)

The son of an architect and pupil of the painter Jacques-Louis David and the architect Antoine-François Peyre, he won the Grand Prix de Rome in 1807. After four years at the Villa Medici in Rome, he travelled in Asia Minor, Egypt, and Greece, where he designed classical triumphal arches, from 1817 to 1822. After he returned to France, he was appointed professor of history and architecture at the École Royale des Beaux-Arts; he was also elected to the Académie des Beaux-Arts.

Guillaume-Abel Blouet (1795–1853)

This descendant of Mansart who worked in Delespine's studio won the Prix de Rome in 1821. He travelled to Italy and Greece, where he took part in a scientific expedition to the Peloponnese. Appointed architect of the Palais des Thermes in Paris, he restored and extended the Château de Fontainebleau and its gardens. After finishing the Arc de Triomphe in 1836, he went to North America to study the new penitentiaries being built in the United States. Made a member of the Institut de France in 1850, he also designed tombs (including those of Vincenzo Bellini and Casimir Delavigne).

Jean-Nicolas Huyot, graphite drawing by Heim, 1829 (Paris, Musée du Louvre).

Caricature of Guillaume-Abel Blouet from *Album de 73 portraits-charge aquarellés* by Louis-Léopold Boilly. Manuscript, 19th century (Paris, Bibliothèque de l'Institut).

Jean-Arnaud Raymond, engraving by Charles Normand (Paris, BHVP).

Publishing director
Dominique Seridji

Publications coordinator
Denis Picard

Assistant publications coordinator
Karin Franques

Editorial coordinator
Anne-Sophie Grouhel-Le Tellec

Translator and copy editor
Chrisoula Petridis

Graphic design and layout
Régis Dutreuil

Production coordinator
Carine Merse

Photoengraving
APS-Chronostyle, Tours

Printing
Mame, Tours, France

Acknowledgements

The author would like to thank the administrator
of the Arc de Triomphe and his team for the interest
they have shown in this project.

© Éditions du patrimoine
Centre des monuments nationaux
Paris, 2007
Dépôt légal: November 2007
ISBN: 978-2-85822-977-2

Photographic credits

Illustrations, cover, and opening pages

Cover: view from the Avenue de la Grande-Armée façade.
Page 19: Bonaparte on horseback receiving the captives.
Detail of *The Battle of Aboukir* by Gabriel-Bernard Seurre,
known as Seurre the Elder (1795–1867). Upper relief, south-east
pier. Facing Avenue des Champs-Élysées.
Page 66: a winged genie with Egyptian clothing and headdress
engraves the heroic deeds of the Egyptian expedition
in hieroglyphs. Detail of *The Return of the Army from Egypt*
by François Rude (1784–1855).
Right section of the side elevation, Avenue de Wagram façade.